Next Level Teaching

To order call 256-759-7492 or visit www.jeremyanderson.org

Published by: Spirit Reign Communications & Publishing

Edited by: Ruthie Jorgensen

Cover Design: Nikita Sarkar

Inside Layout Design: Nikita Sarkar

ISBN: 978-1-940002-98-9

NEXT LEVEL TEACHING

TABLE OF CONTENTS

NEXT LEVEL TEACHING

ACKNOWLEDGEMENTS

I knew that in order for this book to be successful,
I would need to put together a team of educational
experts and professionals who would ensure that
I was adding true value to the lives of the academic
professionals for whom this book was written. My focus
group is made up of teachers and principals from middle
schools and high schools across the country. The goal in
assembling this focus group was for them to challenge me
in my writing and theories on this topic. Their sacrifice and
contributions to this project were instrumental in helping me
formulate my thoughts and theories.

To Ebony Frazier, Frances Tolbert, Darrian Tanner,
Erin Holden, Kia Henley , Ryan Manning, Ms. Q. Morrow,
Erin Tolbert, Martez Gerard Favis and Ruthie Jorgensen.
THANK YOU!

Last but not least, I must thank my wife, Traci,
and daughter, Jewel, for their patience and for allowing
me to fly on a weekly basis to speak life to the many
schools I've been fortunate enough to partner with.
Thanks for your willingness to share me with the world.

INTRODUCTION

You might be asking, what is Next Level Teaching? My wife, Traci, is the president of our non-profit organization, Next Level Living, Inc. The purpose of Next Level Living is to help people from all walks of life pursue the Next Level of their lives. I've had the privilege of traveling and speaking with teachers, principals, and superintendents across the globe. I've spoken in elementary, middle, and high schools from the east coast to the west coast, in Canada, Bermuda, and the Grand Cayman Islands. I've even spoken in over twenty youth detention facilities, and also alternative schools.

In my travels, I've noticed that educators from all walks of life are struggling in the classroom. I've spoken to hundreds of teachers and many have expressed to me that they often struggle to rekindle the fire and zeal they once had for teaching. When they first started teaching, it was enjoyable and fulfilling. Then they later realized that their real life experience in the classroom wasn't quite what they expected. It's a sad reality but sometimes the school that hires you can take away the educational innocence of some teachers. I just left Louisville, KY, where I did staff training for one of their underperforming middle schools in Jefferson County. I was shocked to see that over forty-percent of their teachers were first year teachers. As I looked in the eyes of these teachers, it was clear they weren't really prepared to be placed in what many would say is the most challenging school in their county.

The world is rapidly changing due to technology. We relay thirty to forty percent of our daily communication with others through text, email or social media platforms. The students' attention span is getting shorter while the school days are getting longer. With the growth of social media and technology, many educators today are really struggling to reach this new generation of millennial students. Others are struggling just to get through the day.

The mental anguish of dealing with unruly, disrespectful students is too much for many teachers to handle. Whoever expected there to be such a thing as teacher-bullying?

Since 2010, I've had the humbling privilege of speaking in over forty school districts and training teachers in over 120 schools. When my presentation is complete, and the teachers find out that I've written six books, the number one question I get is, "When are you writing a book specifically for teachers?" I decided to write Next Level Teaching because I have seen the needs of students through my own educational experiences. I have reflected on my own life as a student and I have discovered that there is much that educators need to know. My goal was to write a book that would speak directly to educators and address some of the common issues they struggle with across the globe.

The reality is that teachers need all the help they can get! There are several factors that students are dealing with, such as bullying, teen pregnancy, suicidal thoughts, pornography, and several other things that can be major distractions to students. Another thing we must consider is the number of students who are being molested or are witnessing domestic violence in their homes. Children are being exposed to drugs and pornography at a much younger age than they were ten years ago. All these factors can and will affect the way a child performs in school. In order for us to give these students the best fighting chance, we as educators have to take our interaction with them to the next level. As their world gets worse, educators must get better. We must create a classroom environment much like a haven where the children feel that they are welcomed, respected and understood.

Though I am not a teacher in the classroom, I stand beside you as an advocate for education. You might be wondering, what makes me qualified to write a book to teachers? For starters, I wrote the beginning of the book from the perspective of a once broken and troubled student. I feel I have a special vantage point because of my past and personal experiences along with the hundreds of schools I've spoken in, and the thousands of teachers I've trained. Principals and Superintendents bring me to their districts or schools to boost the overall morale of their staff, or to give training in the areas of burn-out, how to connect with troubled students, how to understand your students, how to build allies in the classroom, how to reach the seemingly unreachable students, just to name a few. This book will hopefully encourage you on your teaching journey as you face day to day struggles in communicating with your students. I also hope that this book challenges you to go to that Next Level so that we can be the best version of ourselves, so that we can help our students to be the best version of themselves.

In the first few chapters of this book, I share with you my journey through school so you can see the power that you have with even the most troubled of students. After my struggles in elementary, middle and high school, I went to college and received my bachelors in social work. In a sense, social work has given me the tools I need to understand the everyday lives of students who come into your classroom every day, and I have mastered how to meet them where they are. This is an important component to teaching as well. I can't tell you how many teachers I've been able to hug as they cry on my shoulder and share the struggles of teaching and the burden in the classroom. This book was necessary because you, the teachers, are necessary. I wouldn't be who I am today if it weren't for the many Next Level Teachers I've been fortunate to have. The concepts you will read about are my opinions based on my own experiences in the classroom as well as my reflections as an adult of what could have helped me. I wrote this book to inspire and motivate you to reflect on the way you cultivate the next generation in hopes that you will go from being an average teacher to a NEXT LEVEL teacher.

Chapter 1
THANK YOU

CHAPTER 1
THANK YOU

To every teacher reading this book, thank you! Thank you for taking the responsibility of being one special adult whom children interact with outside the home. You have the power to help them succeed. Thank you for being a hero.

I remember September 11, 2001 like it was yesterday. I was in my dorm, Edwards Hall at Oakwood University. I was channel surfing looking for some sports updates when the channel stopped on a news station. It was then that I saw the second plane hit the twin towers of the World Trade Center. To my horror, like most Americans, I thought what I was seeing on my television screen was a movie. I soon realized that our country was under attack. What shocked me almost as much as the attack itself was the actions of the first responders.

I watched news stations show live footage of brave Firemen & Policemen in New York City running fearlessly into buildings filled with smoke. As people ran out of the buildings, they flew straight toward the danger to aid anyone in need. I often compare educators to that level of bravery. The average person from the outside looking in complains about how bad the school districts are, or what rough shape their school is in. They complain about how this new generation is lost but do absolutely nothing about it. You Next Level educators, on the other hand, didn't sit back and complain about the problem, you ran into the profession of teaching.

The courageous Policemen & Firemen of NYC received adequate training for major emergencies and attacks, but there is nothing that could have prepared them for the level of tragedy that occurred on September 11, 2001. It is the same with educators.

"YOU MIGHT BE GOING THROUGH A **DIVORCE,** HAVING FINANCIAL ISSUES, HEALTH ISSUES OR OTHER CHALLENGERS, YET YOU SHOW UP **EVERYDAY PREPARED** TO GIVE YOUR ALL BY SERVING THESE **STUDENTS.**"

You got your schooling, completed your practicum, took the PRAXIS and received your Bachelors/Masters and PhD's. Even though you made the educational investments and did all the necessary prep work, there are some things you just can't learn until you get in the classroom. And let's not forget that you're human, so you have your own personal issues to deal with daily. You might be going through a divorce, having financial issues, health issues or other challenges, yet you show up every day prepared to give your all by serving these students.

Thank you for selflessly giving your time and energy to educating our future leaders. You yielded to the calling of teaching and have dedicated your life to leading this new generation into greatness. Thank you for every student you demonstrated concern for over the weekend. Thank you for every student you bought lunch for. Thank you for every time you had to go into your own pocket to purchase supplies for your classroom. Thank you for being the mom, dad, counselor, and cheerleader to your students. Thank you for your willingness to be overworked and underpaid. Thank you for sacrificing your own health and sanity for hundreds of students who may never say thanks. Thank you for continuing to work hard so you can hear the "Thank you" from the one student who will actually say it.

Thank you for giving students your shoulder to cry on. Thank you for taking advantage of those teachable moments. Thank you for the times when you tutored during your lunch break. Thank you for taking one lesson and making it apply to different students and their personalities. Thank you for not letting the classroom know you were having a bad day. Thank you for the times you hid your tears with a smile. Thank you for every cheesy joke and funny song you gave students to make difficult subjects easy to learn.

Thank you for every whip and nay-nay you attempted with the hopes that the dance would build you some credibility and relationships with the students. Thank you for not giving up on that, seemingly, hopeless student. Thank you for the successful and unsuccessful attempts at building relationships with the parents of your students. Thank you for believing in your students when some of their parents didn't believe in them. Thank you for the amazing things that you do every day, often without a simple THANK YOU.

Average Teachers: Do enough to say that they're doing their job. They tend to stick to the lesson plan only.

NEXT LEVEL Teachers: Are courageous enough to do what needs to be done to reach their students.

Chapter 2

MY
STORY

CHAPTER 2
MY STORY

If there was ever a student who would make you second guess your calling to be a teacher, I was that student.

I was the type of student you hoped caught the flu over the weekend so he wouldn't be in class on Monday. The type of student that when I missed class, you thought that was a gift from God. The type of student that every teacher in the school would talk about, in hopes that my name wouldn't land on their roster for the next year. Diagnosed with Attention Deficit Hyperactivity Disorder (ADHD) and a sense of humor that was sure to land me on comedy central, I was a teacher's worst nightmare. I had the unfortunate gift of drawing attention to myself and taking control of the classroom. Every day, it seemed as though it was a showdown between me and my teachers to see who would command the attention of the students. I took so many trips to the principal's office. If there had been a point system for how many times per week I would be in the principal's office, I would've had frequent flyer miles or some kind of platinum medallion status by eighth grade. Simply put, I was a hyperactive, untamable terror. I knew my teachers thought I was a terror by their facial expressions, and by the way they would talk to me. I could feel their frustration and negative energy towards me.

Although I was a bit of a terror in the classroom, I was not a bad kid. I was mainly just misunderstood. The way I would respond to my eclectic home life was by being disruptive in class. My mother was only sixteen years old when she gave birth to me. She did the best job she could to raise me. Even though I had my issues; bad attitude, short attention span, class clown and being a slow-learner (most of which came from my ADHD diagnosis), my mother has always been my number one supporter. She is by far the strongest woman I know.

My mom got married when I was 8. After the wedding I remember asking my dad, "Are you going to be my daddy?" His answer was yes! He's been my hero ever since then. He never treated me like a stepson, nor did he ever call me his stepson. I grew up in a pretty nice home. My parents worked hard to provide a loving home for me and my siblings. It's obvious, however, that the absence of my "biological father" had a negative effect on me. I was the oldest of four children so I naturally developed leadership skills early on.

I was born in the 1980s, and during that time, America was still trying to understand ADD/ADHD and how to deal with those diagnosed with these disorders. For my teachers, it was an easy fix. Their solution for controlling me was to give me Ritalin every other hour. The medication calmed me down but, in some ways, turned me into a zombie. Instead of being encouraged to find healthy ways to help channel my energy, my prescribed dosage of medication was doubled.

Middle School

As I got older and transitioned from elementary school to middle school, my behavior got worse. I would disrupt class with my jokes, talking or spit balls. I was also disrespectful to my teachers. At the end of the day, I wanted attention. My behavior in class would cause me to frequently visit the principal's office. Although I had a mom and a dad in the home, both parents worked all day so I didn't get the academic attention and nurturing that I needed at home. I also had three other siblings who needed my parents' attention as well. My mom did the best she could but the reality is that with her giving birth to me at the tender age of sixteen, she was just a child herself. The attention I was yearning for at school evolved from the attention I desired at home. Soon, I was completely out of control. The schools tried everything they could to discipline and control me. If it wasn't In-School Suspension (ISS), it was after school detention, then suspension and ultimately expulsion.

"THEIR SOLUTION FOR CONTROLLING ME WAS TO GIVE ME RITALIN EVERY OTHER HOUR."

Growing up, my family moved around quite a bit. From the fourth to seventh grade, we moved from Dallas, TX, to Plainfield, NJ, to East Orange, NJ, and then to Huntsville, AL. You can imagine the negative affects this had on me. There were times when I'd experience a sense of normalcy for a while, only to be uprooted at the end of the year for a new city and state. With every new school I attended, the process of being liked and accepted started all over again. It's always hard being the new kid in school, and that's what fueled my determination to be liked and accepted. The easiest way for me to feel accepted was to make people laugh. I figured that if they laughed they would like me, and if they liked me they would accept me. So with every new school, I would assume the role of class clown. My parents made a desperate attempt to place me in a more nurturing school environment when we arrived in Huntsville, Alabama. My dad worked extra jobs so that my family could afford to put me in a private Christian academy starting in eighth grade. Our family absolutely could NOT afford this, but again, it was a desperate attempt to place me in a school where I could feel accepted and nurtured.

Like every school I had attended before, I made my mark by making a name for myself. After an extremely rough eighth grade year, my year ended with me being identified again as the class clown. This time it was so bad that my eighth grade teacher, Mr. C, actually sat my mother and father down and began to give them reasons why they should leave me behind to repeat the eighth grade. The words "He won't make it in high school" and "He's not high school material" actually came out of his mouth. My parents, like most parents would do, ignored his unfortunate and negative opinions about my capabilities. Against my teacher's recommendations, they decided to send me off to high school.

High School

My mother had a lot of faith in me. Faith is the substance of things hoped for, and the evidence of things not seen. So when my mother saw me, she saw the best in me. Even though my behavior

THE WORDS "HE WON'T MAKE IT IN HIGH SCHOOL" AND "HE'S NOT HIGH SCHOOL MATERIAL" ACTUALLY CAME OUT OF HIS MOUTH.

said one thing, she chose to believe something else. I hate the fact that I let her down on a continual basis. Then there were people like family members, classmates, and past teachers who did not believe in me, and unfortunately my behavior proved their opinions of me to be true. This is one of my main messages that I share when I speak to students in schools. Next Level Living is about proving those who believe in you right, while proving those who don't believe in you wrong. I wish I had known then what I know now. I went into ninth grade with my hyperactive guns a-blazing. This time I felt like I was on a big stage, so I had to make my presence known and really make a name for myself at this new school. I was so successful in marking my territory at this new school that I began to do a series of pranks that would rock the whole school. I became pretty popular around the school, and with every successful prank, the word began to spread that I was behind them. This made my popularity grow even more. As a freshman, I had the attention and respect of everyone in the school, even the juniors and seniors.

I'll never forget the day I successfully executed what I thought was a purely genius plan. This was on the level of the movie Oceans 11. I say that because it was a group effort. The mission was to turn off the electricity in the school so that school would have to be dismissed. In addition to this, the juniors were taking a major exam that period that they weren't enthused about taking. I knew that a successfully orchestrated mission of this nature would put me in even better standing with the upper-class men. The plan was simple: I had one classmate distract one of the main custodians while another student swiped his keys. Then I had another student create a diversion that would allow me to slip out of class. Once I successfully escaped the classroom, I made my way to the main utility closet that held the main power generator that powered the whole school. The only problem was I had to go through what seemed like 100 keys before finding the key that unlocked the door. After a few minutes of frantically trying key after key, finally, the door opened. I knew that once I shut the power down it would take hours for the system to reboot. Now my only problem was which lever would shut the power off in the whole school. Could it be the lever that was marked 'MAIN' in red letters? I gave it a pull and suddenly the whole school went dark.

As soon as the school went dark, I put both my fists in the air like I had just won a championship boxing match. I thought this was such a smooth plan. I felt like I had stolen $100 million dollars from Caesars Palace Casino in Las Vegas, Nevada. Everything went according to plan until the whole school began to chant my name. JERE-MY, JERE-MY, JERE-MY, JERE-MY! Oh no! I thought. My popularity in the school gave me away. Those who I sought to please ended up giving me up. I wanted their cheers and applause but not out loud. Within minutes, I found myself in the principal's office, and within the hour my mother was back at the school.

As a result of my ingenious, well thought out and perfectly executed plan, the school kicked me out. The school my parents sacrificed and worked extra jobs to get me in, said that I was too much of a pain and hassle. After getting kicked out, I went to another local public high school that was walking distance from my house. It was one of the worst schools in the city. Needless to say, things for me got worse. This school was so big and there were so many students there that my teachers didn't even care if I was in class or not. Every day, I hung out with the so-called "cool kids." All they did was go to skip parties, have sex, get drunk and get high. That year, because of my behavior and absence from school, I completely failed the ninth grade. My whole world changed on the last day of school. When my home room teacher handed me my report card, I realized that my absence in class resulted in me getting F's in every class except P.E., which I at least scored a C in.

Updated Report Card

After all the pain and hell I put my parents through, there was no way I could come home with this report card. I spent the last period of the day panicking and day dreaming. Then it came to me!

"I STILL REMEMBER TODAY HOW GOOD THAT FELT TO HAVE MY MOTHER SAY THAT SHE WAS PROUD OF ME."

I came up with another ingenious plan, or so I thought. Since I didn't like my grades, I would simply change them. After school, I took my report card, which was paper back then, and made my way to the library. I took some whiteout and blotted out all the F's, and the one C. After the whiteout dried on the paper, I took a fine point pen and put those tiny dots on the paper to give myself all A's, and two B's. I then went to the copy machine and made a copy. I gave it a very critical eye. I was impressed with my work! This was like a scene from the widely popular movie, Catch me if you can, starring Leonardo DiCaprio.

The plan was complete, all I had to do now was see if my mom would buy what I was about to try and sell her. As soon as I walked through the front door questions began to fly my way. "Why are you home so late?" "What have you been doing?" "Where's your report card?" I began to shake and stutter, not knowing which question to answer first. With sweat rolling down my face, I just handed her my report card. She took one glance at it and asked a question that made my heart stop, "Why is this a copy? Where is your real report card?" Thinking quickly I said, "Mom, that is it. Somehow, I lost my original report card so they made me a copy of their master copy in the office." She then started examining the report card and shaking her head. After thoroughly scanning the report card she looked up at me with tears in her eyes. She then followed up with the words I'd been waiting to hear for a long time, "I'm so proud of you!" That moment, even though it was based on a lie, felt good. I still remember today how good that felt to have my mother say that she was proud of me.

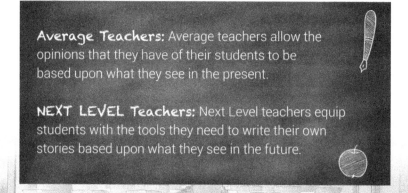

Average Teachers: Average teachers allow the opinions that they have of their students to be based upon what they see in the present.

NEXT LEVEL Teachers: Next Level teachers equip students with the tools they need to write their own stories based upon what they see in the future.

JOURNAL

What adjustments can you make
to take your teaching to the
Next Level?

_____

_____

_____

_____

_____

_____

_____

_____

_____

_____

_____

_____

_____

_____

_____

_____

_____

_____

_____

_____

_____

_____

_____

_____

_____

_____

_____

_____

_____

_____

_____

_____

_____

_____

_____

_____

_____

_____

_____

_____

_____

_____

_____

_____

_____

_____

_____

_____

_____

_____

MY STORY

Chapter 3

SPEAK LIFE

CHAPTER 3
SPEAK LIFE

So there I was, going to a third school for the ninth grade. Being kicked out of the private Christian academy hurt my mom, but what hurt even more is going to the second school and failing there too, and then lying to her about it...again. With concerns about the environment of the previous school, my parents enrolled me at Huntsville High School. This school was approximately fifteen minutes across town from where my previous school was located. This school was different. Here I had what I would call some "crazy" teachers. I call them "crazy" because they were saying new things to me like, "Jeremy, you have so much potential" and "Jeremy, you can achieve great things." This type of talk was foreign to me. They were being overly optimistic and positive while affirming me as a student.

The great King Solomon once said that "Life & Death are in the power of the tongue..." It's been proven that when you hear nice and affirming things, you naturally feel good. The same for when you hear negative things. Those comments make you feel bad. There are studies that have proven that negative energy and words can kill plants, and that plants that had nice words played to them grew and flourished. The environment, nutrients, and soil were the same; the only difference was the words. I remember working for a corporation where one of my managers was extremely negative. The morale within the office was very low. After six months of mental torture from this manager's depressing, negative comments, the company moved him to a new location. They replaced him with a new manager and the environment in the office changed almost immediately. Not only did my co-workers and I feel good about our job and the environment, but our performance also increased. The same can and will take place in the classroom. The energy that you give off can make all the

"THE GREAT
KING SOLOMON
ONCE SAID THAT
"LIFE & DEATH
ARE IN THE
POWER
OF THE TONGUE..."

difference in your classroom, and the lives of your students.

Faith factor

I was so used to teachers being negative towards me that being at this new school seemed weird. The ethos and culture within the school was warm and inviting. Some of my teachers were nice and very positive. They spoke life to me, meaning they affirmed me and only spoke positive things about me and the other students. It was like music to my ears. The reality is that I was a young, immature kid who sought any king of attention I could get, and the attention I received was positive and affirming. Their positive words were foreign to me. Before long, I was willing to do whatever I needed to do to get them to continue. It was as though these teachers, unlike the ones at the previous school, really cared about me. The words they spoke sounded so good but were honestly hard for me to believe. To this day, I wonder if they really believed what they were saying to me. This is where our faith in these kids must kick in. You see, when you have faith in something, and you believe in it, you start to respond to the situation differently.

I believe that in order for you to be a Next Level Teacher, you have to have a certain amount of faith. Did my teachers know that I would grow up to be a homeowner, faithful husband and devoted father, business owner, author of six books, and a successful public speaker? I don't think so. I think their faith left the potential of my future up to their imagination. What if I told you it's not up to you to believe in your students. You just need to believe and the impossible can happen in their lives. When I speak to students, I can't control what they do a year down the line, but I can control what I speak over their lives at the time. I make sure I tell the students that I have faith in them and that I'm expecting the best from them. I believe that the words I speak to students are seeds that I plant in their hearts and souls. It is then up to you as teachers to nurture and cultivate those seeds with your words and deeds until they blossom and become fruitful.

SPEAK LIFE

29

"I BELIEVE THAT THE WORDS I SPEAK TO STUDENTS ARE SEEDS THAT I PLANT IN THEIR HEARTS AND SOULS."

If you could be a fly on the wall in the homes of some of your students your heart would break to hear what is spoken over their lives, oftentimes by their parents. "You're dumb as nails." "I'm tired of taking care of you." "You're going to be just like your father." "I wish I never had you." "If you weren't born, things would be so much easier." "What's wrong with you? Are you stupid?" Imagine a kid who lives in a home where they hear remarks like that from their parents on a daily basis. Now, think of the kids who deal with the verbal abuse from their family only to come to school and get bullied by other students as well. For some of your students, the classroom isn't just a place to learn but a refuge of safety and hope, so choose your words wisely.

They changed my life

My new teachers at Huntsville High School literally changed my life. I know it sounds like a cliché, but it's my reality. Regardless of how I acted, my teachers spoke life into me on a consistent basis. What happened was a miracle. I started to believe what they were telling me! When I first heard the positive comments, I just thought they were trying to be nice or polite, but as the words of affirmation continuously came my way, I slowly began to believe what they were telling me. Their consistency liberated me from the bondage of the previous negative mindset that tried to control my life. Even on the days when my behavior was disruptive, they would say things like, "Jeremy, I expected better from you. You're a leader. I know you can do better. Try to focus harder next time. You are extremely smart, and you have a bright future. I believe in you." That was big! I was used to my parents being the only people who believed in me. To hear my teachers' expectations for me pushed me to turn their words into my reality.

I always wondered what made these teachers different from teachers in my past. Why did they care so much when the others couldn't have cared any less? Was it the environment? Were the teachers at the urban school burned out from working at a school where ninety to ninety-five percent of the students came from low income homes? Were my current teachers less stressed because this school had a population that consisted of more students coming from middle and high income homes? Was it because these teachers were happy, and the other teachers weren't? Did the location of the school make a difference with one in the low income part of town and the other in a more affluent area? Whatever the reason was, the seeds these teachers planted began to grow.

Let's get Involved

A couple of my teachers suggested that I get involved with other activities within the school. I felt like it was a joint effort on their part. I could tell that they were sharing notes with each other about me. Reluctantly, I took their advice. The first thing I did was enroll into the Jr. ROTC Program, which gave me some additional order and structure. I also joined the Sigma-Psi-Phi Academic fraternity, which helped me stay focused on my academics. One day, when I should have been in class, I was caught flirting and chasing a girl down the hallway. As I turned the corner, I bumped into one of my teachers. I ran smack into his plump belly. Upon impact, I fell directly to the floor. He stood there over me with a smile and said, "Jeremy, you've got some speed on you. I'll give you two options, either you can meet me in the principal's office, or you can meet me on the track field after school." And just like that I joined the track team.

To make a long story short, that year I completely turned things around in school. I got B's & C's, and my family was pleased. I finally had it together. That summer, I went to summer school, and the following year when the regular school day ended, I took night classes and caught up to my proper grade level. The first private school that ended up kicking me out let me return. Not only did I graduate from high school on time, but I was also a part of the student government and I was nominated chaplain in my senior class. After graduating from high school, I went on to go to college and pursue my bachelors in Social Work. If those teachers had not spoken life into me on a consistent basis, there is no telling where I would be. The faith that my new teachers had in me made them treat me with respect and give me the positive attention I so desperately desired and deserved.

Average Teachers: Tend to be bound by perception. They categorize their students by their mistakes of the past. They lack the imagination and faith needed to believe in their most troubled students.

NEXT LEVEL Teachers: Next Level Teachers speak life to their students, regardless of their behavior. They "choose" to see the best in the students they've been entrusted with.

JOURNAL

What adjustments can you make

to take your teaching to the

Next Level?

Notes

_____

_____

_____

_____

_____

_____

_____

_____

_____

_____

_____

_____

_____

_____

_____

_____

_____

_____

_____

_____

_____

_____

_____

_____

_____

_____

_____

_____

_____

_____

_____

_____

_____

_____

SPEAK LIFE

Chapter 4

CREATING ALLIES WITHIN THE CLASSROOM

CHAPTER 4
CREATING ALLIES WITHIN THE CLASSROOM

As educators, we should never underestimate the power of peer to peer influence. There are some students who have the power to influence other students' thoughts and behaviors, especially when it is time to be attentive in class. They are able to take the floor and make their peers laugh by being disruptive or they speak out of turn in class with a voice almost as overpowering as an adult. When I was young, I was that student. There were two leaders in the classroom and, depending on the day, either the teacher or I would rise as the victor by the final bell. I wasn't necessarily trying to take over the classroom, it just happened naturally. I noticed that when I acted up, I would get the attention of my teacher, and I loved it. At the end of the day, that is what I longed for. If you have these types of students in your classroom, you actually reward them by giving them the attention in exchange for their distracting behavior. Although the attention is negative, to them it is still a win. Since we know that attention is what they desire, we should change the culture by giving them attention publicly for the positive behavior and privately for negative. This distinction will keep you as the teacher in control of the situation. When a minor interruption occurs, redirect the class to get back to work, then get close to the student and quietly ask him or her to step into the hall. Have the student stand across from you where he or she cannot be seen by the rest of the class, and you stand in the doorway. This allows you to continue to monitor your other students while taking the power away from the disruptive student. This also gives the student the opportunity to reflect on his or her actions without the audience of peers to feed off. If the behavior continues, try talking with the student during an activity that he or she enjoys, like P.E. Controlling your emotions is key to successfully reaching the student.

"CONTROLLING YOUR EMOTIONS IS KEY TO SUCCESSFULLY REACHING THE STUDENT.

You don't want to be the one who becomes frustrated because of the child's conduct, the child should be the one frustrated because of their own actions

The Guilt Trip

The guilt trip is a technique that teachers used on me when I was in school, and I have trained other teachers to use it in their classrooms as well. During my problem years in school, I noticed that behaviors that would typically upset my teachers eventually ceased to have an effect on them. It was as though they began to ignore me and my disruptiveness. If my behavior really got out of hand, they would pull me aside in the hallway and say something like, "Jeremy, I'm disappointed in you. I can't afford for you to distract the other students so I must send you to the principal's office. I really don't want to do this but if I keep allowing this to happen then it's not fair to your fellow classmates. I really like you, and it makes me sad when you have to leave my classroom. I believe that tomorrow you can have a better day." WOW!!!! This hit me to my core. For starters, the teacher did not give me the attention in the classroom. This conversation took place outside in the hallway, which saved me the embarrassment of being scolded in front of my peers. Also, she stated that she "liked" me. That was a new feeling for me. I was convinced that all of my previous teachers disliked me, and I couldn't blame them.

Knowing that my teachers actually liked me made me feel guilty when my behavior wasn't good. I started wanting to hear them say things like, "You had an awesome day today, Jeremy, I'm really proud of you." Instead of showing me attention when my behavior was bad, my teachers only showed me attention when it was good. You can probably imagine what began to happen. I worked hard every day to make sure that I could hear those words of affirmation. I began to build relationships with my teachers, and class after class my behavior began to change for the better.

Another tip that could work within your classroom is rapport building activities. Building rapport or relationships with your students will help them to understand that you care about them as individuals. Find out what activities they like. For example, if they like sports, toss a ball around with your students, and allow the person who catches it to share a highlight from his or her weekend, holiday or the day before. This activity allows students to express themselves by talking about a topic of their choice. This can also be helpful in getting some of the low performance students to share things, in general. Once they become accustomed to sharing ideas in front of their peers, you can incorporate the ball or object into your lessons. You can use it as a tool to determine who answers a question or who leads the discussion.

Identify Your Spy

I will never forget the day I became a spy. As the relationship between this specific teacher and I grew, she began to give me small responsibilities in class. One day, she pulled me aside and asked if I would be her secret leader. I laughed and said, "You want me to be a spy?" She laughed as well and said, "If that's what you want to call it." She then began to tell me how the kids in the classroom looked up to me and how I was a natural leader. I thought the offer was quite flattering, but I wasn't sure if I knew what she expected of me. She explained that she just needed me to set the example. When things got out of hand with the other kids, she wanted me to use my voice and influence to encourage them to act right and cooperate with her. I was all in. I liked the idea of being a secret agent. This was my first time positively nurturing my gifts as a natural born leader.

I'm sure this seems like a risk, but you might be surprised at what happens when you give power to the students who are already fighting for it. The students in your class who give you the hardest time will often grow up to be some of the most influential leaders. The type of environment they progress through will determine the type of leader they will become. If they grow in a positive environment, they will become the type of leader who gives back to society and makes it a better place.

"THE STUDENTS IN YOUR CLASS WHO GIVE YOU THE HARDEST TIME WILL OFTEN GROW UP TO BE SOME OF THE MOST INFLUENTIAL LEADERS."

However, if their growth is stunted in a negative environment, then they will probably be the kind who makes their society or community worse. Once you identify who these students are, they can prove to be potential allies within the classroom. You will want to go through the steps you learned in the last chapter and speak life to them. Then you will be able to gain their trust, and once they know that you really believe in them, and that you are for them and not against them, they'll be more willing to help you in the classroom.

Policing Themselves

Once you've identified who in the classroom are your more troubling students, and have taken a few weeks to really work them through relationship building, then you're ready to invite them to be the unspoken leader in the class. Best case scenario, your new unspoken student leader will be a major help bringing order in the classroom. Worst case scenario, your student will begin to police his or herself, and that alone is huge. Even if they don't gain the respect, cooperation and order from their peers, the fact that they are not causing you extra headaches and pain is huge!

These students are great to use in classroom settings/activities or labs. The students can serve as demonstrators for portions of the activity as long as you feel that you can trust them to set the right examples. Interestingly enough, students tend to pay more attention to their peers, but if the student volunteers and is on "your side" the observing students might just accidentally learn something from that demonstration. Now you're working smarter, not harder! Soon their cooperation will be noticed by the class, and then you'll see that shift take place, which can create a new culture within the classroom. Kids are smart, they'll probably notice a difference and some will follow suit. These students will soon emerge as being leaders without even trying to be.

Average Teachers: Tend to look at the students who give them the most trouble as the enemy. They fail to see them as students who are troubled but have the potential to be leaders.

NEXT LEVEL Teachers: Accept the challenge of reaching their most troubling students. They are intentional about building relationships with them, and see these students as flowers waiting to bloom.

JOURNAL

What adjustments can you make

to take your teaching to the

Next Level?

Notes

_____

_____

_____

_____

_____

_____

_____

_____

_____

_____

_____

_____

_____

_____

_____

_____

_____

_____

_____

_____

_____

_____

_____

_____

_____

_____

_____

_____

_____

_____

_____

_____

_____

Chapter 5

FORMING ALLIANCES WITH PARENTS

CHAPTER 5
FORMING ALLIANCES
WITH PARENTS

O ne of the number one questions I get is, "How do you build relationships with parents?" This is vital if you plan to have a long lasting effect on that student's life. One thing that I know for sure is that I did not want my mother and my teachers talking. I wanted to keep what I did in the classroom completely separate from my home life. If my behavior in school got back to my mom, I knew I was in deep trouble. Little did my teachers know that if they would have reached out to my mother, she would have played a vital role in the improvements in my classroom behavior. I can only imagine how it would have been if my mother and my teachers built a relationship. Developing a relationship with the parents of your students can prove to be beneficial. Since this will take time, energy, and effort, you may want to make it priority to connect with the parents of your most challenging students.

Parents who are Receptive

Building relationships with the parents of your students must be initiated by you. Parents love their children and will bring you the very best that they have. They can sometimes be very defensive when it comes to discussing their children. You should initiate the process of becoming allies early on in the school year. After all, you are the captain, and the classroom is your ship. You might want to start the conversation off something like this: "Hello, Ms./Mr. Tanner, my name is Ebony, Ryan's ninth grade math teacher. I believe some really great things will come from Ryan, and I would love to touch base with you from time to time so that we can work together to ensure Ryan gets the most out of this year. Do you mind if I send you weekly updates and progress reports for him? Also, feel free to share with me anything that you think I should be aware of so that I can best serve Ryan."

As you build relationships with parents, they will begin to give you insight into the child's strengths and weaknesses. As the trust builds, the parent begins to share family dynamics with you. This will help you in connecting with the student. You will be able to find special ways to relate to them as well. The information that the parent shares with you should remain confidential, but it is important that the student knows that you have direct contact with their parent or guardian.

Once the relationship is established, the parent or guardian may then give you the inside scoop to what's going on with the student. You will find that a partnership will begin to form. Before you know it, the parent will call, email or text you things like, "Hey, Ebony, Ryan spent the weekend with his dad and they had a falling out. Just wanted to give you a heads up, he's still really upset about that." Well, once you get this intel, you'll know what approach to take with Ryan when he comes to class. Without this intel you'll be left with assumptions as to why he was quiet or uncooperative, but now because of the relationship you've built with his mother you know that Ryan had issues with his father. You also know that Ryan's parents are either divorced, separated or just don't live together.

Parents who aren't Receptive

There are times that you'll find a direct correlation between the parents who aren't initially receptive and the students who seem to present you with the most challenges. If you didn't already know, when you tell the parents that their child is having issues they will automatically feel that you are attacking their parenting skills. They will feel as though you believe they have failed as parents. This even happened to me. My wife and I enrolled our daughter, Jewel, in a private school because I knew they would accept her into Pre-K early. She didn't turn four until October, and when we met with her teachers halfway through the year, we were crushed to hear that she might not be ready for kindergarten. I actually sunk into a slight depression that evening and began to

"AS YOU BUILD RELATIONSHIPS WITH PARENTS, THEY WILL BEGIN TO GIVE YOU INSIGHT INTO THE CHILD'S STRENGTHS AND WEAKNESSES."

blame myself for not doing extra work with her after school. Was I a bad parent? Of course not, but I took it personally knowing that my daughter wasn't performing on the same level as the other kids. Although she's the youngest in her class, I still questioned my parenting. We're referring to a little girl who is an only child and lives with both of her parents. Think about the single mother you will be speaking to, who might have two jobs and multiple kids. She's doing the best that she can do, and after the initial conversation, no matter what you say she will still feel that she failed. Considering this, you'll want to be tactful with how you approach the parent so that she (or he) can let her (his) guard down.

Most of the parents that you speak to who are reluctant, should be approached in a tactful manner. You don't want the parents to feel that their child is bad, and that's the only reason you want to stay in touch with them. You'll want to let them know that you long for a relationship/partnership with them so that you can best serve and teach their child. *"Hey, Mrs. Ewing, my name is Jennifer, and I'm Erin's history teacher. Erin is a great child, and I am confident that if we work together, we can help her be even better. I would like to stay in touch with you to share the good things that Erin does in class. I would also like to get ideas from you on how to help Erin when she has difficulties. I am here to help you and Erin have the very best experience at our school."*

How to communicate?

There are several ways you can communicate with the parents or guardians. First and foremost, you should always do what is most comfortable for you. Boundaries are key, so if you aren't comfortable with them having your personal cell phone number to call or text, then you should consider having them call the classroom phone during your planning period. Maybe email is best for you. There are several text messaging apps that provide an alternative phone number as well. Whatever it is, make sure that parents are aware of the lines of communication. Send weekly reports home in a sealed envelope. Make the parents feel as though you are

"MAKE THE **PARENTS FEEL AS** THOUGH YOU ARE **PARTNERS WORKING TOGETHER** IN AN EFFORT TO DEVELOP THE POTENTIAL **YOU** SEE IN THEIR **CHILD.**"

partners working together in an effort to develop the potential you see in their child. Always start conversations with something positive and then gradually introduce the areas of concern. It is also beneficial sometimes to only share the positive. Parents are more prone to answer calls and return messages if they know that you share as much good news as you do bad news.

It is imperative that you have these conversations with the parents. The reality is that the majority of your students know how they should behave in school. Some of them act differently at home and treat you a certain way because they feel they can get away with it. Your students know that their parents wouldn't allow some of the behavior that is shown in your classroom. Sadly enough, in some homes the house is in worse shape, with multiple kids there. You'd be surprised at the number of households there are where the parents aren't even present, and the children are left to fend for themselves. In these cases, that unruly behavior presented within your classroom is a cry for order and structure. Children want to know that they are loved and safe. If you can create an environment where these types of kids feel as though they can let their guard down and be kids, you will win them over. This is why it's important to see what your students' home life is like and the relationship with the parent, or the lack thereof, can give you some insight into that.

At the end of the day, you aren't just seeking to build a relationship with the parents; you're looking to build a partnership. You both should have one thing in common, and that's the success of their child, your student. I believe that partnerships help all parties involved. The parents will begin to see a change in the behavior at home because this communication will bring common structure between home and school. You, as the teacher, will also benefit because you'll soon see the behavior change in the classroom, and the student will gain the most because they will know for sure that you and their parents are working together just for them. This will increase the value and worth that the student feels personally about him or herself. Sometimes it's the small efforts that can make the most difference.

Average Teachers: Tend to complain about parents who are hard to work with, and deem that as the reason that their students aren't performing well.

NEXT LEVEL Teachers: Seek out the opportunity to build relationships with the parents of their students, and will form a partnership to help the student/child reach their fullest potential.

JOURNAL

What adjustments can you make
to take your teaching to the
Next Level?

_____

_____

_____

_____

_____

_____

_____

_____

_____

_____

_____

_____

_____

_____

_____

_____

_____

_____

_____

_____

_____

_____

_____

_____

_____

_____

_____

_____

_____

_____

_____

_____

_____

_____

_____

_____

_____

_____

_____

_____

_____

_____

_____

_____

_____

Chapter 6

TRULY KNOWING YOUR STUDENTS

CHAPTER 6
TRULY KNOWING
YOUR STUDENTS

This is probably one of the most important chapters in this book. If you can't understand your students, then how do you expect them to understand you and what you're teaching them? Truly knowing your students is one of the most challenging parts about being an educator. With so many personalities, ethnicities, backgrounds and cultural differences, how on earth are you supposed to teach them?

This is why I have so much respect for educators. You all are challenged to do a mental balancing act with the child, adolescent and teenage versions of our future leaders. In addition to the personalities, backgrounds and cultural differences, you also have different maturity levels in the classroom. In this chapter, we'll take a look at the different learning styles of your students, as well as exploring some of the personality types that they have. Once you understand this, you'll be in a better position to really connect with them, which will help in their understanding of your lesson plan.

Learning Styles

Let's just highlight the fact that each of your students have different learning styles. Knowing their style of learning is just one component to knowing them. Some of your students are visual learners (spatial), so they do better using pictures, images and spatial methods. Some of your students learn by auditory stimuli (aural). These students prefer using sound and music, while others are verbal (linguistic), so they do better using words in speech and writing. Some of your students learn by practical and physical examples (kinesthetic) meaning they would rather use their body, hands, and sense of touch to grasp a concept. Some students learn best during Solitary (intrapersonal) moments, so they prefer to work alone, while others are Social (interpersonal) where they thrive by learning in groups or with other people.

"YOU ALL ARE CHALLENGED TO DO A MENTAL BALANCING ACT WITH THE CHILD, ADOLESCENT AND TEENAGE VERSIONS OF OUR FUTURE LEADERS."

Then you have those students who are logical (mathematical), and those students learn best when they apply logic and reasoning.

Not every student learns the same. Most students use several of the learning styles such as the ones listed above in order to grasp concepts in the classroom. Some visual learners may also be interpersonal learners, while some interpersonal learners may have a clearer understanding of how each student learns. This is the key to knowing the student. Some of these styles will be evident the more time you spend with your students, while others are hidden. Sometimes, the parents can give you insight as to what the learning style of their child happens to be. This is why building relationships with the parents is key. As you begin to gather and share knowledge on the student, it gives you both better chances of reaching your goals in the classroom and the home.

My favorite teacher was Mr. West. He understood my classes' learning styles and adjusted his instruction to fit them. One major strategy he used was competition. He knew that my classmates and I learned by doing interactive, hands on (kinesthetic) activities. He held competitions on Fridays. He would split us into two teams, give each team a buzzer, and ask us questions two by two. Whoever buzzed in and answered the question correctly earned a point for the team. This activity made learning fun and exciting! My team wanted bragging rights every week, so we went home and studied in order to win on Friday. This strategy taught my classmates and me three things. The first thing we learned was team work and collaboration. Secondly, we were motivated to study. Lastly, it gave us an incentive to behave. If anyone acted up, we lost our privilege to compete.

Personality Types

Knowing your students' personality type is important as well. Are they choleric (extroverted, outgoing, bossy, easily angered), sanguine (extroverted, positive, happy), melancholy (introverted, sensitive, sad), or phlegmatic (calm, introverted, unmotivated)?

Knowing this will better explain why they make choices they do in the classroom. Now you may or may not be able to give a personality test to your students, but paying attention to different personality traits can help you to identify who might fit within certain categories. Many of the teachers I've coached in the past haven't given that much thought to the learning styles and personalities of their students. Who really has time for that when you have a classroom filled with unruly, obnoxious kids all demanding your attention and the attention of their peers? It's seemingly impossible to break down and understand the socio-economic status of each student while teaching them in their preferred learning styles, but it can be done. One student at a time. It just takes intentional work.

I had a teacher by the name of Mrs. King-Jordan. I'm not sure if she knew everyone's personality type, but she definitely knew mine. She understood that I was an extrovert who did not want to be embarrassed in front of my peers under any circumstances. She also knew that I struggled a little bit in her class. She would give the entire class an assignment, and once everyone started working she would say, "Hey, Jeremy! Will you come help me with something?" Once I got to her desk, she would give me one on one instruction to ensure that I understood the material and could do the work.

A friend of mine by the name of Martez Favis, always went above and beyond to meet the needs of his students. Each year, he would develop a theme in his classroom based upon the personalities of his students. One year, he had an all-boys class and a sports theme, which included a basketball in the back of the room. He would use that goal as a reward for getting answers correct in class during oral reviews. Each correct answer gave his students the opportunity to shoot the basket for prizes. His students loved it, paid attention in class because they wanted the opportunity to shoot the basket. The purpose for this chapter is not to necessarily tell you how to teach them in a way that can coincide with their learning styles, but more so for you to have a clear understanding of how delicate each and every student can be. Every single student of yours is a precious, sensitive, soul that is complicated to say the least. The reality of your classroom is that you have some students who could be taught by a robot. Literally. They could watch a teacher virtually instruct them on the smart board, receive assignments and do just fine or better. There are other students who need more practicality and relatability to their instruction. While both types of students are equally represented in a classroom, both learn differently and require different methods of instruction.

The E.R.

I'll never forget doing staff training at a school. After my fifty-minute presentation, I did a Q&A session where one teacher said to me, "Mr. Anderson, it sounds like you're saying that we shouldn't treat the students the same. I don't think that's fair." In my response, I told her that I totally understood where she was coming from. I then asked her a few questions. I said, "Is it fair that Stacy is being molested by her stepfather? Is it fair if Madison just lost her younger sister in a car accident? Is it fair that Randal's mother is an alcoholic and his father is in prison? Of course not." I then proceeded to ask, "Should they be treated like the other students who come from perfectly loving homes or do they need a little extra attention considering their circumstances?"

I view the classroom like a hospital. Some children come in and they're dealing with a tummy ache or maybe they need to get a prescription filled. They need to see a doctor, but they are willing to wait a few hours while other patients with more severe and life-threatening situations are seen ahead of them. Would you make the person who had a heart attack wait like the person who might be suffering from a toothache? Of course not. Both people deserve to see the doctor and will see them, but the victim who was in the car accident needs a little more attention than the person who has a rash on their arm.

"ALL OF YOUR **STUDENTS** DESERVE YOUR **ATTENTION,** BUT IN ORDER FOR SOME OF YOUR STUDENTS **TO HAVE A** FIGHTING CHANCE, **THEY NEED A** LITTLE MORE CARE AND ATTENTION **FROM YOU.**

The same goes for the classroom. All of your students deserve your attention, but in order for some of your students to have a fighting chance, they need a little more care and attention from you. Some of your students will go home to parents who care about their school day and want to hear all about it. Their family will gather around the dinner table together and eat, talk about their day and then do homework together. Then you have other students who are being verbally abused and have to find and make dinner for themselves and three younger siblings because their mother is nowhere to be found. This is their reality. This is why your students are fortunate to have educators like you who care enough to go the extra mile to find out their learning styles and personality types, all in an attempt to provide the best learning experience in the classroom.

Average Teachers: Teach the curriculum given, and struggle to find the time to really get to know their students.

NEXT LEVEL Teachers: Go above and beyond to reach their students. They are intentional about understanding their most troubled students and believe that they can first build trust, then a relationship with the student.

JOURNAL

What adjustments can you make

to take your teaching to the

Next Level?

Notes

_____

_____

_____

_____

_____

_____

_____

_____

_____

_____

_____

_____

_____

_____

_____

_____

_____

_____

_____

_____

_____

_____

_____

_____

_____

_____

_____

_____

_____

_____

_____

Chapter 7

GAINING RESPECT IN THE CLASSROOM

CHAPTER 7
GAINING RESPECT IN THE CLASSROOM

One thing that is clear is that there is no set physical re - quirement to be a teacher. You can be short or tall, big or small, male or female, young or old. All you need to have, besides the training, is a passion for the students. It's interesting to see how a 30-year-old teacher who's six feet, two inches tall can have a class that is completely unruly and out of control, while across the hall there's a 60-year-old lady who stands a mere four feet, eleven inches and her class is silent. Controlling your students in the classroom all boils down to one thing: How you earn and give respect.

Create the Culture

Culture within the classroom is just as important as setting the right culture within a corporate organization or sports team. The same reason that some football franchises are successful and others aren't has less to do with the players and everything to do with the culture of the organization. Take the New England Patriots, for example, they are one of the most successful football franchises today. They have won nine of their thirteen conference championship games. In addition to that, they've won five of the nine Super Bowls they've played in; 2002, 2004, 2005, 2015 and 2017. That's impressive!

It's clear the New England Patriots have successful winning seasons year in and year out. The pattern of their success begins at the head and makes its way down. The Coach, Bill Belichick, is a serious, no nonsense coach. He doesn't tolerate disrespect, showing up late to practice, distractions or any of the other foolishness other head coaches tolerate. He's known around the NFL as being a fair, straightforward coach who expects nothing but the best from his players. When new players join the team, they know the system in which they're joining. It's imperative for you to create the

"CULTURE WITHIN THE CLASSROOM IS JUST AS IMPORTANT AS SETTING THE RIGHT CULTURE WITHIN A CORPORATE ORGANIZATION OR SPORTS TEAM."

culture within the classroom. Make sure that the students know that your classroom is a classroom filled with winners. If they want to win, then they will follow your rules, and if they don't want to win, then the proper adjustments will be made.

Setting Clear Boundaries & Rules

Everyone loves a goofy, fun loving teacher. While we need more of those, it is especially important to set clear boundaries within the classroom. So while you are being personable and fun with the students, they should also know that there are lines they just don't cross or there will be consequences. Make sure that they have a clear understanding of what your expectations are of them. Make it known what you will tolerate and what you won't tolerate. Maybe you can even give them something to sign, kind of like a contract. When they act up, you tell them that they broke the contract, and according to the terms of the contract, their punishment is X, Y, or Z.

It's important to know that how you start is how you will finish. I suggest you start the school year off in a fun-loving way, but set the tone that you will not tolerate any disruptions or disrespect. Instill within your students that you all are a team, and that you have to always operate and function as the team. No player is bigger than the team. So often when students are being disruptive in the classroom they are thinking only of themselves. When you use language like (us, we, team,) they tend to feel more accountable for their behavior. The student should be able to see core values and/or rules posted somewhere in the classroom. This will serve as a physical reminder of what you and your classroom stand for.

Take Command

Order in the classroom has nothing to do with the size of the teacher, but more so the size of the teacher's command. I've seen classrooms where the teacher gave their power over to me or another student because they failed to take command of the class.

"ORDER IN
THE CLASSROOM
HAS NOTHING
TO DO WITH THE
SIZE
OF THE TEACHER,
BUT MORE SO
THE SIZE OF THE
TEACHER'S
COMMAND."

I've seen students go toe-to-toe with their teachers in arguments. Let me be clear...this is a fight for power. These conversations would have died had they been in private. You might need to pull the student out of the classroom and into the hall or office. When this type of reprimand takes place in the classroom and the student has an audience, then power slips out of your hands with every word that is exchanged.

A good way to handle an unruly student in the classroom is to wait one-to-five minutes after the distraction, and invite the student outside. However, there are some situations that will need to be dealt with right there on the spot. As we learned in the previous chapters, we don't want to give attention to the negative things. We do, however, want to publicly acknowledge the positive things the student has done. This shows the class what meets with your approval and what is worthy of your praise. This is another way of invoking your power and authority in the classroom. Everyone loves praise and recognition, so when you make a habit of celebrating when one of your students "scores" or "earns points" it's a win for the whole class.

Give Respect Gain Respect

If you ask a student what the number one thing is that they want, many of them will tell you they just want to be respected. If you can instill within your students the power of earning respect, then you'll see a drastic change in their behavior. Let them know that the respect that they desire is the same respect that must be given. Many of the students aren't used to being held accountable for what they "say" they want. They "say" they want respect but might not give respect. It's your responsibility to teach the students who cause the most distractions, that they are required to give respect to themselves, to you and to their classmates.

Here's a scenario: One of your students has a loud outburst in class and then curses at another student. Here's an opportunity to apply what we learned above.

"IT'S YOUR RESPONSIBILITY TO TEACH THE STUDENTS WHO CAUSE THE MOST DISTRACTIONS, THAT THEY ARE REQUIRED TO GIVE RESPECT TO THEMSELVES, TO YOU AND TO THEIR CLASSMATES."

"Hey, Megan, can you meet with me for a moment?" As you and Megan walk outside, you close the door and ask her these questions, *"What's going on? Are you ok? What was that all about?"* After she gives you whatever her excuse is, your response can be, *"Today, you violated several things in our agreement. We are a team, and it's my responsibility to hold you accountable as a team member. Today, you didn't show respect to me because you broke one of my rules. You didn't show respect to yourself because I know you can do better. You didn't show respect to your classmates because you disrupted class. Now, did you notice how I called you outside to address this as opposed to doing so in front of the whole class? I did that because I have respect for you, and I expect that you should have the same respect for me. Is that too much to ask?"*

Here the student is seeing a few things: A) They broke the rules of the classroom. B) They disrespected themselves, the class and you. And, finally, C) you still showed respect to them even though they didn't offer you the same courtesy. You will, however, have students who want to go back and forth with you and will blame the other person. Students like that will take more time to deal with. Oftentimes, depending on the student's maturity level, they'll be unable to understand the power of being responsible for how they respond. One thing I try to instill into the hearts and minds of students today is that, "you can't control what happens to you, but you can control how you respond."

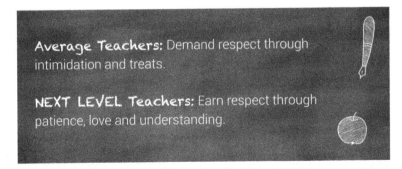

Average Teachers: Demand respect through intimidation and treats.

NEXT LEVEL Teachers: Earn respect through patience, love and understanding.

JOURNAL

What adjustments can you make
to take your teaching to the
Next Level?

_____

_____

_____

_____

_____

_____

_____

_____

_____

_____

_____

_____

_____

_____

_____

_____

_____

_____

_____

_____

_____

_____

_____

_____

_____

_____

_____

_____

_____

_____

_____

Chapter 8

BE RELEVANT

CHAPTER 8
BE RELEVANT

While learning about difficult concepts such as math or science, you've often heard your students say, "When am I ever going to use this in real life?" Relevant learning is truly effective learning. Relevancy is what this new generation is looking for. Most of the students I've spoken to across the country don't see how relevant education is in a practical world. It's bad enough that they don't value education. Most students today don't quite understand why they need to know what it is you're trying to teach them. The best educators in the world are the ones who can apply practical applications to their lesson plans.

The difference between the educational system and typical lesson plans today, as opposed to thirty years ago, is that it's the same message taught with a new method. We've got to find more ways to connect with students on a relevant level. In the previous chapter, we looked at the importance of gaining respect in the classroom. But what about the students' respect for the lesson plan within the classroom? If we don't help our students find relevancy in the lesson plan, then they will either forget the information as soon as they learn it, or they will be disengaged from the beginning. From middle school up, I didn't view what I was learning as important information. If I did, I would have been more engaged during the teachings.

Be Practical

Some of the best communicators in the world have mastered the art of storytelling. They know the value in painting pictures through verbal illustrations, and assisting in helping your imagination merge with the point of their message. This helps those in the audience grasp the concept so that they can understand the theory in a practical way. This is an important tool in the class-

"STUDIES HAVE SHOWN THAT WHEN YOU'RE PRESENTING THE LESSON IN A PRACTICAL WAY, IT INCREASES THE STUDENT'S INTEREST AND WORTHINESS OF THE SUBJECT."

BE RELEVANT

room while sharing the lesson plan. This will also help to keep the students' attention.

Studies have shown that when you're presenting the lesson in a practical way, it increases the student's interest and worthiness of the subject. You want to be sure that the student feels you genuinely want them to grasp this knowledge so that they can be successful later in life. When you take the practical approach, the students' guards will be down, and they'll be more interested in what you're sharing with them. When you share with your students, you want to share with them how this topic, subject or lesson plan helped you. Tell them what you were able to accomplish by knowing this information. This helps them to see you in a practical way, and their connection to you will give them the desire to view the material in a more practical way.

Have fun with it

Who says teaching can't be fun? And who said you can't have fun while teaching? Some of you teachers are with your students eight hours a day. You might as well enjoy the time you have with them. The best classrooms are the ones where the students are engaged with one another in group discussions. Maybe prizes can even be given to the group that gives the best explanation to the lesson plan.

One good practice for your students is to share with them the concept or lesson in the first half of the class period. Then ask them to write a page or half page on how they can apply this to everyday life, now or in the future. Then go around the class and have them share. Sometimes the students will be shy and won't want to share in front of their peers. In this case, you could collect the papers and read the top answers. This will get your students thinking for themselves. Then you're able to come in and share with them your thoughts on the topic. The benefit of this is that you're getting your students to share amongst themselves, and they are getting knowledge from you. This will help them further their understanding or correct their misunderstandings.

My friend, Martez, took having fun to the next level when he transformed his classroom into a recording studio. The theme for this particular year was ROCKSTARS, which was an acronym for Rising Over Challenges & Keeping a Strong-willed Tenacious Attitude while Reaching Success. The students recited this statement every morning as a reminder of the work they were doing over the course of the year. In addition to the theme, Mr. Favis helped his students turn popular songs into study guides. They wrote and recorded "piggyback" songs to help them learn and review science and social studies content. Some of these songs can be found on SoundCloud by searching for Mr. Favis. He didn't just stop there, he also allowed his kinesthetic learners to create dances to go along with the songs to engage them in the process as well. He definitely had a way of keeping learning relevant. He is currently an Assistant Principal at a performing arts school.

Keep it Current
One of the most beautiful things that you can do in the classroom is give some examples of what's happening in the world to drive home your point. Maybe you're trying to get them to see how the government works. You can talk about the recent election or what's currently happening in the senate, and how important it is to know how government works. Maybe you're teaching a math class; you can talk about the economic condition of a company, or you can look at the financial situations in your local city and state. This will help them see the importance of being well-informed in the areas of finance and money.

Another idea is to have some guest speakers from time to time who can drive home the point of the lesson plan. Of course you can't have a speaker every week, but every so often this can be something that can help you connect in a relevant way to your students. The speakers should be people who either work in that industry that is tied to your lesson, or maybe someone who can

"MAKE IT A HABIT TO INSTILL WITHIN YOUR STUDENTS THE IDEA THAT THE WORLD NEEDS AND DESERVES THE BEST VERSION OF THEM."

share a real life experience that they had that would further prove the point of your lesson plan. The student will then see the true value in what you're sharing, and this will help them remember the principles as well.

The key is for the students to see that, every day, the world is happening around them. The sooner they see how the world works, the sooner they can make positive contributions to this world. Make it a habit to instill within your students the idea that the world needs and deserves the best version of them.

Average Teachers: Tend to stick to the curriculum only and are limited in their connection with their students.

NEXT LEVEL Teachers: Do what's necessary to remain credible and relevant in the classroom.

JOURNAL

What adjustments can you make
to take your teaching to the
Next Level?

_____

_____

_____

_____

_____

_____

_____

_____

_____

_____

_____

_____

_____

_____

_____

Chapter 9

PUT YOUR OXYGEN MASK ON FIRST

CHAPTER 9
PUT YOUR OXYGEN MASK ON FIRST

I am on an airplane flying to places where I speak and train at least once a week. Living in Atlanta, which is Delta Airlines' main hub, allows me to catch direct flights to every major city in the U.S., and other countries. I travel so much that I could probably pick up a part time job for Delta as a flight attendant. To anyone who has been on an airplane, you've heard the classic line, "In the event of an emergency, an oxygen mask will automatically appear in front of you. To start the flow of oxygen, pull the mask towards you. Place it firmly over your nose and mouth, secure the elastic band behind your head, and breathe normally. Although the bag does not inflate, oxygen is flowing to the mask. If you are traveling with a child or someone who requires assistance, secure your mask on first, and then assist the other person."

I'll never forget flying with my daughter thinking, "NO WAY!" If something goes wrong I'm putting her mask on first. After conversing with my wife and a few friends I began to understand a little more of the importance of putting my mask on before my daughter's. The theory behind this suggestion is that if you don't first take care of yourself, you will not be any good for the person next to you. I think that the same principle applies to teachers in the classroom. You're already overworked and underpaid. On top of that, you don't know how to turn it off. You bring your work home with you, and it can even at times have a negative effect on your home life. You carry a lot, and I'm here to help lighten that load.

You Carry a Lot
I wrote this section for those of you who don't truly understand the importance of taking care of yourself. When I do assemblies and speak to the student body, I always make a point of helping the students view you, their teacher, as a human being.

"BELIEVE IT OR NOT, MOST OF YOUR STUDENTS DON'T SEE YOU AS HAVING A LIFE OUTSIDE OF THE SCHOOL."

Beleive it or not, most of your students don't see you as having a life outside of the school. Many of them think you live in the school. Literally, it's as if your classroom has a secret door that gives you access to a bedroom, with a shower and sink. I can't tell you how many times I've spoken to students and said, "You do know that your teacher has a life outside of school, right?" And the reply is a weird, puzzled look on their face.

I'm sure you've experienced something like this: You're at TJ Maxx, and you run across one of your students. With a shocked look on their face they said, "Hey, Mrs. Tolbert, what are you doing here?" And you replied, "Shopping." They went to school the next day and told their classmates that you were spotted in TJ Maxx in a sweat suit. To them, the fact that you shop, eat, go to the bathroom and sleep, is weird but to you it's the norm. In reminding the students that their teacher is, in fact, a real person, I inform them that you also have feelings. You and your spouse could have marital issues, you could suffer from depression, and you could be diagnosed with cancer.

The human side is the side that they need to see. You are expected to drive to the school every day and leave all of your problems, issues and concerns in the car. You have to be a mother, father, counselor, therapist, and teacher for your students. It is safe to say that you carry a lot! It's time for you to carry less so you can find a better balance that will make you whole. You cannot give students what you do not have. If your life is full of chaos, anger, and frustration, that's exactly what you are going to pass on to your students. If all you do is yell and scream at home, that's what you're going to do at school.

The Best of You

Your students deserve the absolute best of you. If you are off, your classroom will be off. When I do staff trainings at various schools, the number one complaint I get from staff members is that they're burned out. I attribute this burnout to the fact that most teachers

"YOUR STUDENTS DESERVE THE ABSOLUTE BEST OF YOU. IF YOU ARE OFF, YOUR CLASSROOM WILL BE OFF."

PUT YOUR OXYGEN MASK ON FIRST

go above and beyond in and out of the classroom. While being fully committed to your students is a good attribute, you're actually doing more harm than good. If I was a flight attendant, I would recommend that you put your oxygen mask on first.

This new generation of students are up against many things their parents were not at their age. In order for them to have a fighting chance, they need the best version of you; the sharp, insightful, funny, refreshing, thought-provoking teacher that you are. Most of the teachers who experience mid-year fatigue would admit that when they first started the school year, they were on fire. Then that fire soon burned out. It is mostly because of not taking time for self. There is only one you. The truth about education is that if you died today, there would be a replacement for you soon after. You must do what is best for you physically, mentally and spiritually so that you can be the best version of yourself for your students.

Body Mind & Soul
I've found that the weekend is the best time for you to refresh and reboot your body, mind and soul. For your body, working out, walking, jogging or running can be a good stress reliever. You'd be surprised at how getting the blood flowing on a Sunday morning can help jumpstart your week. If cardio isn't your thing, then maybe you'd consider joining a gym? This can be a good place for you to take out the frustrations from the past week at school. Another thing that can help you refresh your body is to be mindful of what you feed your body. Your body is a machine and needs the best fuel.

Everyone loves comfort food, I enjoy my share of pizza and cheesecake from time to time, but I suggest you enjoy these in moderation. It's a no-brainer that your physical health has a direct effect on your career. Not only does it affect your career it also impacts how you process information and feel inside. I don't want to come off as a dietitian, but fresh fruits and vegetables, water, and less fast food will have you feeling better and stronger, and this will have an effect in the classroom and in your life.

When it comes to protecting the mind, there are different ways you can protect it. There are times when I'm home with my girls and the phone and computer are off. I need that mental time to shut down, sit back on my sofa and enjoy some football, a Disney movie with my daughter, and a few hours of HGTV with my wife. I make it a point to almost shut down from extra work responsibilities. This helps me stay fresh when I'm on the road traveling and speaking. It could be different for you. Maybe it's a good book, some home shopping network, fishing, or some other hobby that you enjoy. Whatever you do, find a way to disconnect from the hustle and bustle of the classroom and enjoy your downtime.

As far as the Soul, for everyone it will be different. For me, it's church, and hot yoga. I know, I'm just full of surprises. If you know me, you know I'm a man of faith, so that's one way I take care of my soul, but hot yoga? That is truly next level. I'll never forget being in Montreal, Quebec for a speaking engagement, when my host invited me to his wife's hot yoga studio. It was the most refreshing, relaxing experience I've ever had in my life. It was so amazing that I fell asleep on my mat after class. I was supposed to be working on my breathing, then my breathing turned into snoring. It was so refreshing that when I came back home from the trip, I tried to convince my wife to commit to joining me weekly. So, whether it's a local church or charity organization where you volunteer, or you do yoga or some other form of meditation, make sure that you take care of your soul.

You deserve it. Go get yourself a massage or a mani/pedi. I'm not ashamed to say that I get massages. At least four times a year. I need that time to relax and de-stress. I used to think it was weird, but now I find value in that because I found value in me. I pour out so much on a weekly basis, that I need that time to pour back into myself, and you should too. So on the weekends, make sure you pour into yourself so you have something to pour into your students.

Average Teachers: Either do just enough to get by in the classroom, and have no issues with R&R, or they go the extra mile for their students but they fail to take care of themselves with a proper work/life balance.

NEXT LEVEL Teachers: Have a healthy balance of going above and beyond for their students, but also prioritizing the time needed for them to take care of themselves. They know that their students will only be as good as they feel.

JOURNAL

What adjustments can you make

to take your teaching to the

Next Level?

_____

_____

_____

_____

_____

_____

_____

_____

_____

_____

_____

_____

_____

_____

_____

_____

_____

_____

_____

_____

_____

_____

_____

_____

_____

_____

_____

_____

_____

_____

Chapter 10

YOU DIDN'T SIGN UP FOR THIS!

CHAPTER 10
YOU DIDN'T SIGN UP FOR THIS!

I can't tell you how many times during my one-on-one sessions, I've had teachers recite this classic line to me, "I didn't sign up for this." Often times, this statement is presented with tears flowing from their eyes. They got to a point where the weight of teaching and the other many expectations became a bit overwhelming for them. At this point all I can do is hug them and let them know I understand. It's OK to cry! Crying and releasing your frustrations are healthy ways of dealing with your emotions. Considering all that you've gone through, your tears or warranted! Most of the novice teachers that I work with tell me that their training didn't prepare them for how they're expected to perform in the classroom. Many colleges teach outdated strategies and curriculum that leave first year teachers at a disadvantage. This lack of training causes many young teachers to leave the field of education. It's my hope that this chapter will help some of you hang in there.

All of the above

The reality is that many teachers today are expected to go far beyond the curriculum. From the teachers I've interviewed over the years, they say that in addition to being a teacher, they feel they have to also be a mother, father, and counselor for their students. If a student lacks love and attention from his/her mother, he/she is naturally going to desire it from you. That's human nature; when we lack something we automatically look to fill that void in other areas. This longing for love and attention holds true in fatherless homes especially. If the father is not in the home, the student will look to his male teacher, if one is available. In most instances, this is not the case and students look to older males they know. These males can be positive or negative influences, and they have power to affect the lives of these male students forever. This is why your job as a teacher is so important.

"NEXT LEVEL TEACHING IS GOING BEYOND TEACHING WHAT'S ON THE LESSON PLAN AND MEETING THE INDIVIDUAL NEEDS OF THE STUDENTS."

Many of you have already experienced this desire for human connection. Needless to say, since these students spend more time in school than they do at home, they long to have a strong connection with you. Now some of you may be thinking, 'They don't pay me to be their mother, father or psychologist.' Trust me, I get it. But Next Level Teaching is going beyond teaching what's on the lesson plan and meeting the individual needs of the students. I've seen situations where the teacher makes the student feel that they care, and it's made all the difference. Your students come from all walks of life where they may or may not feel loved. Some special attention and affirmation can go a long way. I know this from personal experience. Some of the best teachers I've had, and have been privileged to work with, were able to teach me the curriculum and still build personal relationships with me. They asked me how things were going at home. They empathized with my situation and told me how proud I made them. This went far...very far.

Walk in their shoes

I'll never forget speaking at a school in Alabama where I was working with their staff on morale. During our staff training, one of the new teachers (who was a Caucasian female around thirty years old) blurted out the statement, "I just can't relate to these kids." After her statement, I noticed other teachers softly nod their heads in agreement. My response to her was that, I understand that you don't relate to them. The problem is that you don't care to relate to them. It is not the kids' responsibility to relate to you. As the educator and the adult in the picture, you have to find ways to relate to them.

Spend a day in their shoes and see how they're living. Consider facilitating a home visit and see what their home life is like. That will tell you a lot about their performance in the classroom. Can you change things in the home? Probably not. But this knowledge will give you a better vantage point when working with that student in the classroom. We need less sympathy, and more empathy. Don't just feel bad for some of your underprivileged students but understand their pain. This is what doctors do. When you go to the hospital the doctor ask you the reason for your visit. Then he or she asks you what symptoms you are having and runs tests on you. After the questions and tests, they diagnose and prescribe the medicine needed for your specific case. The doctor isn't trying to be nosey, he or she knows that in order to properly treat you, they need to have a clear understanding of what your issue is. We need to do the same for our students.

Teacher / Detective

I know you're probably thinking... 'Jeremy, are you asking me to be a Private Investigator or a Detective?' No, I am not. I am asking you to care. Care enough to find clever ways that you can get information from your students. Care enough to do some fact finding. Care enough to see that something is wrong, and know that you can do something about it. You have opportunities to bring mental shifts in the minds of the students in your classroom, especially those who are performing at lower levels academically. I believe that some of the best teachers are nosey teachers. Get into your students' business. Know their likes, dislikes, fears, and successes. This information will help you gain their trust and loyalty. There's an old saying that states, "Students don't care what you know until they know that you care." This is Next Level teaching.

Let's be honest, because of social media platforms such as Snapchat, Instagram and Twitter, this new generation of students DO NOT TALK face to face. You can ask them questions but they're like a closed book. This is what I would suggest in order to get information from your students. Give it your own personal spin but create an environment in the classroom, where students feel comfortable opening up to you about their lives. Some teachers are doing a "Looking forward to Friday." They go around the classroom on Friday and let each student share with the class what they're looking forward to over the weekend. Others do the same thing on Monday, but they share something cool that they did the past weekend.

"GIVE IT YOUR OWN PERSONAL SPIN BUT CREATE AN ENVIRONMENT IN THE CLASSROOM, WHERE STUDENTS FEEL COMFORTABLE OPENING UP TO YOU ABOUT THEIR LIVES."

When students share their experiences, it gives you, as the teacher, an opportunity to find out more about their world and how they live behind closed doors. So, on Friday when a student says, "I'm looking forward to this weekend because my brother and I are spending the weekend with my dad," that lets you know that he/she comes from a broken home, so maybe this is why the student has been acting differently. A student might say, "This weekend the police came to my house because my mom and dad were fighting." Now you know there could possibly be abuse in the home. What takes place in the home affects the performance in the classroom. So, in order for you to really reach and connect with your students, the depth of your interaction with them must go beyond the lesson plan. If you can embrace the idea that you might need to be all of the above, you'll find a stronger connection to your students. If you're willing to take a walk in their shoes, and understand where they come from, you'll have a better understanding of who they truly are. Lastly, if you're able to do some effective fact finding, you can begin to build an even greater understanding of your students' life outside of the classroom, which will help you inside the classroom.

Average Teachers: Stick to what's in their job description.

NEXT LEVEL Teachers: Go above and beyond to meet the needs of their students.

JOURNAL

What adjustments can you make

to take your teaching to the

Next Level?

_____

_____

_____

_____

_____

_____

_____

_____

_____

_____

_____

_____

CLOSING THOUGHTS

You are amazing, and your life on this earth matters more than you know. You've been tasked with the important job of molding and grooming this new generation of leaders. The future of our world starts in your classroom. You are life-changers, therefore you are world-changers. I look at the impact I've made on a global level, and I'm only one person in my thirties. I wonder what would have happened if the teachers at my third school had been average? I can only imagine the future policemen, doctors, engineers, congressmen & women, even presidents that are being shaped every day in your classrooms. I beg you to love harder on yourself because you deserve it. Then, you'll be able to love your students better. I challenge you to dig deeper into why you became a teacher, and that will help you dig deeper into the purpose of each student. I challenge you to see beyond what the student chooses to show, and see the greatness in them even when they might not see it in themselves. I challenge you to go beyond being an average teacher and to harness the inner **NEXT LEVEL** Teacher within you! Thanks for all you do. Now, let's go change the WORLD!

ABOUT JEREMY

Jeremy Anderson's main goal in life is to help individuals become the best version of themselves. He has been gifted with opportunities to speak to a wide array of audiences across the globe. Whether he's speaking at a school, a church, or a company, Jeremy has the ability to help his audience experience true Next Level Living.

Jeremy's personal pursuit of Next Level Living has taken him from the East coast to the West coast, from the hills of Bangalore, India to the city of Johannesburg, South Africa and all the way to Australia, the land down under. Beyond the speaking, training and the writing, Jeremy is a family man. Jeremy and his wife, Traci, live happily in Atlanta, GA with their daughter, Jewel. When he's not on the road speaking or in the gym working out, he's home playing Barbies with his daughter, or trying out a new restaurant with his wife.

CONNECT WITH JEREMY

@1Jeremyanderson

@1Jeremyanderson

Jeremy Anderson

Jeremy Anderson

Booking@jeremyanderson.org

Jeremyanderson.org

BOOK JEREMY

Jeremy's troubled past makes him the perfect advocate for education. His story of repeated failure in school, a diagnosis of ADHD, drug & alcohol abuse, and low self-worth, is one that resonates with students today.

Topics include:
- **Finding Your Purpose**
- **Decreasing the Dropout Rate**
- **Anti - Bullying & Changing That Culture**
- **Positive Decision-Making Skills**
- **Knowing Your Worth**
- **ACHIEVING & SUSTAINING SUCCESS**

During Jeremy's school presentations, he shares his downfall in life and rise to success. This serves as proof to your students that NOTHING is impossible if you're willing to put in the work. Jeremy has an uncanny way of connecting with the students of any audience in a real and relevant way. His objective is for the students to recognize the power of education so that they can experience Next Level Living!

Visit jeremyanderson.org today!

NEXT LEVEL STUDENTS

Looking for someone who can empower and motivate your students? Well look no further! Jeremy's desire to add more value in classrooms across America has led him to create this video series. Next LEVEL Students speaks to the everyday issues that your students face. Subscribe on YouTube and enjoy the FREE weekly series!

Subscribe on YouTube TODAY!

STAFF
TRAINING

Jeremy recognizes that teachers today are the real heroes, and many times they're overworked and underpaid. The schools that bring Jeremy in to conduct student presentations also contract with him to train their staff. Because of his past, Jeremy can be a valuable asset to your staff and will help them connect with some of their most challenging students. His training sessions with your faculty and staff will give your staff that needed boost to help them experience Next Level Teaching.

Topics include

- HOW TO FIGHT BURNOUT & BOOST MORALE
- BUILDING ALLIES IN THE CLASSROOM
- EQUITY TRAINING
- RELATING TO AT-RISK STUDENTS
- OVERALL MOTIVATIONAL SESSION

Visit jeremyanderson.org today!

ORDER FOR YOUR STAFF

Contact us to see how you can order copies in bulk
for your staff or district at a discounted rate.

GET THE
GEAR

JOIN THE MANY
TEACHERS
ACROSS THE COUNTRY
THAT'S MAKING A
STATEMENT!

MAKE A STATEMENT

ORDER A SHIRT

FOR YOURSELF

OR FOR YOUR

WHOLE STAFF!

Visit Jeremyanderson.org/shop today!

ADDITIONAL NOTES

ADDITIONAL NOTES

_____

_____

_____

_____

_____

_____

_____

_____

_____

_____

_____

_____

_____

ADDITIONAL NOTES

ADDITIONAL NOTES

_____

_____

_____

_____

_____

_____

_____

_____

_____

_____

_____

_____

_____

_____

ADDITIONAL NOTES

_____

_____

_____

_____

_____

_____

_____

_____

_____

_____

_____

_____

_____

SPIRIT REIGN
PUBLISHING
A Division of Spirit Reign Communications